One World

Where We Live

Valerie Guin

FRANKLIN WATTS
LONDON·SYDNEY

**Note
about the series**
One World is designed
to encourage young
readers to find out more
about people and places
in the wider world. The
photographs have been
carefully selected to
stimulate discussion
and comparison.

First published in 2007 by Franklin Watts
338 Euston Rd, London NW1 3BH

Franklin Watts Australia
Hachette Children's Books
Level 17/207 Kent St, Sydney, NSW 2000

© Franklin Watts 2007

Editor: Caryn Jenner
Designer: Louise Best
Art director: Jonathan Hair
Maps: Ian Thompson
Reading consultant: Hilary Minns, Institute of Education, Warwick University

Acknowledgements: Adrian Arbib/Still Pictures: endpapers, 2, 3, 23. Jo Bass/The Advisory
Service for the Education of Travellers, Oxford, 17. Mary Cherry/Holt Studios: 15. James Davis
Worldwide: 10. DCLvisions: 11. L. Fordyce/Eye Ubiquitous: 20. David Forman/Eye Ubiquitous:
25. Robert Francis/Hutchison: 19. Ron Giling/Still Pictures: 12. Martin Jones/Ecoscene: 13.
Wayne Lawler/Ecoscene: front cover. Roy Maconachie/ EASI Images: 16. P.Maurice/Eye
Ubiquitous: 7b. John Miles/Eye Ubiquitous: 21. Ray Moller: 7c. Sally Morgan/Ecoscene: 8.
Tony Page/Ecoscene: 9. Harmut Schwarzbach/Still Pictures: 6. Ariel Skelley/Corbis: 26. Penny
Tweedie/Still Pictures: 22. Julia Waterlow/Eye Ubiquitous: 24, 27. Jim Winkley/Ecoscene: 18.
Nick Wiseman/Eye Ubiquitous: 14.

Every attempt has been made to clear copyright. Should there be any inadvertent
omission, please apply to the publisher for rectification.

A CIP catalogue record for this book is available from the British Library

ISBN: 9780749676568

Dewey Classification: 643

Printed in Malaysia

Franklin Watts is a division of Hachette Children's Books.

Contents

Our homes

Where you live is your home.
Your home keeps you warm
and dry. It is somewhere you
can eat and sleep – and play!

This is a **map** of all the **countries** in the world. All around the world, people live in homes.

▶ This boy is outside a house. It is his home. Read this book to find out about the different kinds of homes that people live in.

Old and new

These old houses are in Italy. They were built about 900 years ago. Since then, many people have lived in them. The insides of the houses have changed, but the outsides look much the same.

These houses in Britain were built only a few years ago. The people who live here use new **technology** to recycle the water they use. They also use energy from the sun to make **electricity**.

Wooden houses

In many parts of the world houses are made of wood. Wood keeps the inside of this house in Switzerland warm and dry in the cold weather.

This house in Indonesia is also made of wood. The sides of the house are open to allow air to pass through and keep the inside cool. The curved roof gives shade from the hot sun.

Flats

Blocks of flats have many separate homes inside. These colourful flats are in Argentina.

Tall flats like these provide homes for the millions of people who live in Hong Kong, a small island in China.

Straw roofs

Roofs can be made of many different **materials**. This thatched cottage in Russia has a roof of straw. The thick straw keeps the house warm.

These houses in Mali also have roofs of straw. Long grass is dried to make the straw. The straw keeps the houses cool and shady.

Decorated homes

People often decorate their homes to make them look special. The women in this village in Burkina Faso worked together to paint these beautiful patterns on their houses.

Travelling families in Britain and Ireland used to live in decorated wagons like this one. This wagon is on show at a traditional Traveller fair.

Houseboats

People who live on houseboats can use their homes to **travel** on the water. These houseboats are travelling on a canal in Britain.

In Vietnam, many people live on houseboats like this one. They travel along the **coast** and up and down rivers, carrying goods from one place to another.

▼

Houses on legs

Some houses are raised up on stilts. This house in the United States needs to be high up so the water will go under it rather than into it.

This house is in the **rainforest** of Indonesia. It is up on stilts so the insects that crawl on the ground can't get inside.

Living in a tent

These people carry their homes with them as they travel through the hot **desert** in Morocco. Their tents give them shade.

People in the cold mountains of Mongolia also live in tents. To keep warm, they make a fire in the middle of the tent. The smoke goes out through a pipe at the top of the tent, like a chimney.

Living in a cave

In northern China, some homes
are built into the side of cliffs.
The front parts of these houses
are made of brick, with big
windows to let in sunlight.

In places in Tunisia, people
dig cave houses down into
the ground. Thick stone
walls keep the cave
houses warm in winter
and cool in summer.

A house is a home

In many homes, families gather together to eat. This family in the United States sits at the kitchen table to have their meal.

This family gathers outside their home to eat their meal. They live in Egypt, where the weather is hot and dry.

All around the world

All over the world, people relax together at home.

United States

Tunisia

Morocco

The countries that you have read about are shown in pink on this map of the world. Find the country that matches each picture in the book.

Argentina

Ireland

Britain

Switzerland

Italy

Mongolia

Russia

China

Vietnam

Egypt

Mali

Indonesia

Burkina Faso

Glossary

coast   where the land meets the sea

countries   places with their own governments

desert   an area of land that is very dry

electricity   a kind of power that can be used to work lights and machines

map   a drawing that shows us where to find places

materials   things used to make other things

rainforest   a kind of forest in a very warm, rainy place

technology   using science to make useful inventions

travel   to move from one place to another

Index